Azure Top Interview Questions and Answers

- ✓ Face the Interview with confidence

- ✓ Helpful for eleventh hour revision

- ✓ 3.Contains Interview Questions and Answers

- ✓ 4.Easy to understand, precise and to the point.

By Mark Tim

~~~

Kindle Edition

Copyright © 2019 by Mark Tim

Kindle Edition, License Notes

Table of Contents:

Chapter 1. Introduction

Welcome to the best Azure stuff I wish you will find here. Start getting ready for next job interview you are going to face. This book covers most likely asked Azure interview questions with a good explanation. Experienced Azure developers share their common interview questions to let you prepare for the technical interview session.

Azure is one of the best emerging cloud technology service. It is one of the comprehensive set of cloud computing services which is widely used by large number of IT professionals and developers for building, deploying and managing the software and hardware architecture of cloud computing applications.

Here is what Azure offers:

- Azure is the only consistent hybrid cloud
- Azure is the cloud for building intelligent apps
- Azure is the cloud you can trust

Questions covered here will help you to approach challenging interviews in the correct manner and with the right attitude.

Confidence is the key towards achieving success. So, to maximizing self-confidence, put your best efforts to show your skills in front of an interviewer.

Just be kind to yourself before attending the interview, and keep saying, all is well and I deserve this job. While attending interview, we all are nervous as it's the time when we have to prepare ourselves for facing the challenges, for giving us a chance to prove our skills and capabilities.

One hour can decide your next step, what you will get and what you actually deserve. Be patient, keep calm, always go for the interview with prior preparation, have basic concepts clear in mind, and do remember,

Success is all results of your courage, self-confidence, your efforts and hard-work.

Keep doing, keep learning, at last it's the knowledge that matters to survive in the job market.

Being the best is not so important,

Doing the best is all that matters.

Chapter 2.

Azure Interview Questions and Answers

Take the time to read the technical and logical concepts every Azure developer must know. I hope you will find these questions useful and below provided list of questions will help you to have quick revision of Azure basic concepts and take you a step ahead towards tackle that interview session

1. Explain the concept of cloud computing?

Cloud computing refers to that elastic computing platform for enabling simultaneous access to multiple pools of system resources and higher-level web services.
Cloud computing offers a wide range of opportunities and capabilities, open a new world covered with flexibility, platforms, services, applications and much more.
Here is listed some of the uses of cloud computing:

- Creating new applications and services in a virtual server.
- Storage, backup and ensures data recovery.
- Hosting of websites and blogs in a global network of virtual servers.
- Audio and video streaming.
- Deliver software's, resources and services on-demand.
- Data analyzing for patterns and broadcasting.

2. What are the different services that are offered on cloud computing platform?

There are basically three services that are offered on cloud computing platform:
- IaaS
  ➢ Infrastructure-as-a-service
- PaaS
  ➢ Platform-as-a-service
- SaaS
  ➢ Software-as-a-service

- IaaS(Infrastructure-as-a-service)

IaaS facilitates to provide IT infrastructure including virtual servers, virtual machines(VMs), storage, networks, operating systems etc. on cloud provider platform on demand basis and thereby pay-to-pay basis.

- PaaS(Platform-as-a-service)
PaaS service facilitates to provide whenever required resources for developing, running, executing, testing and managing a wide range of software applications. It makes easier and quite convenient for developers to quickly create a web or mobile applications without setting up the physical infrastructure.

- SaaS(Software-as-a-service)
SaaS facilitates to provide on-demand software applications on hosted virtual server on demand basis or either on subscription basis for premium requirements. Users will connect to these virtual applications through a web browser on their phone, tablet, PC by connecting the device over the internet.

3. What is Microsoft Azure?

Microsoft Azure is one of the cloud provider for accessing Microsoft infrastructure on cloud computing platform.

Azure is one of the best emerging cloud technology service. It is one of the comprehensive set of cloud computing services which is widely used by large number of IT professionals and developers for building, deploying and managing the software and hardware architecture of cloud computing applications.

4. What are the uses of Azure– Microsoft Cloud Service?

Here are the listed most common uses of Azure– Microsoft Cloud Service:
- Quicker Development
- Autoscaling
- Easier Maintenance and Backup

There are other ten reasons for considering Azure as one of the cloud computing platform:
- Familiarity of Windows
- 64-bit Windows VMs
- Azure SDK
- Scalability and flexibility
- Cost benefits and pricing model
- Data centre in the cloud
- Support resources
- Interoperability

- Security
- Something for everyone

5. What are three main storage and data services provided by Azure?

Three main storage and data services provided by Azure are:
- Azure Cosmos DB
- Azure Storage
- Azure SQL Database

6. What are the ways of using Docker containers through Azure service in your cloud computing applications?

Azure provides several other ways of using Docker containers service in cloud computing applications:
- Azure Docker VM extension
- Azure Container Service
- Docker Machine
- Custom Docker image for App Service

7. What are the authentication ways offered by Azure to prevent unauthorized access to app clients?

Azure provides two common ways to prevent unauthorized access to app clients:
- Azure Active Directory (Azure AD)
- App Service Authentication

8. What are the monitoring options available in Azure - Microsoft Cloud Service?

Here are the listed monitoring options available in Azure - Microsoft Cloud Service:
- Visual Studio Application Insights
- Azure Monitor

9. List the programming language for which Azure SDK is available?

Azure SDK is available for following development platforms:
- .NET
- Node.js
- Java
- PHP
- Python
- Ruby

10. What are different administration roles available to assign during an Azure subscription?

There are three different administration roles available to assign during an Azure subscription:
- Account Administrator
- Service Administrator
- Co-administrator

11. What is Azure App Service Web Apps (Web Apps)?

Azure App Service Web Apps or simply Web Apps is the cloud computing service for hosting set if web applications, mobile applications and REST APIs.

It can be developed in various development platforms including programing languages such as PHP, Python, Java,.NET, Ruby, etc.

While using these app services, it is required to pay for the Azure computing resources that are being used. It depends on the App service plan which is using while operating the web apps.

12. What are the features of Azure App Service Web Apps (Web Apps)?

Here are listed some of the features of Azure App Service Web Apps (Web Apps):
- Multiple languages and frameworks
- DevOps optimization
- Global scale with high availability
- Connections to SaaS platforms and on-premises data
- Security and compliance
- Application templates
- Visual Studio integration
- API and mobile features
- Server less code

13. Name the available roles and what is the use of having these roles?

Roles are just servers that are being managed, load balancing a platform that is designed and developed to achieve a common role.
There are three types of available roles in Azure - Microsoft Cloud Service:
- Web Role
- Worker Role
- VM Role

14. Name the services provided by Azure - Microsoft Cloud Service?

There are various types of service that are provided by Microsoft Azure:

- Web Sites
- Data Management (SQL Database & tables)
- Cloud services
- Virtual Machine
- Business Analytics (SQL Reporting & Data Marketplace)

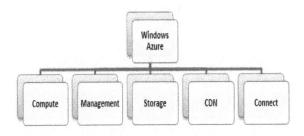

15. Explain the concept of Azure Fabric?

Azure Fabric is a feature of Azure platform, it provides an Azure Fabric Controller service, which is basically an operating system for Azure.

Azure Fabric handles following features:

- All roles and computing resources

- Health monitoring of all computing resources
- Deployment and activating all cloud services
- Allocating, releasing of resources.
- Provisioning Virtual machine, terminating, etc.
- Make use of patches for installed operating system on a virtual machine automatically.

16. What are the main components of Microsoft Azure platform?

Microsoft Azure Platform has three main components:

1. Windows Azure Compute

Windows Azure Compute provides hosting environment and computing services through roles.
It supports three types of roles:

- Web Roles
- Worker Roles
- Virtual Machine(VM) Roles

2. Windows Azure Storage

It provides storage in cloud, through using four types of storage services:

- Queues

- Tables
- BLOBs
- Windows Azure Drives (VHD)

3. Windows Azure App Fabric

It provides following infrastructure services:

- Service bus
- Access
- Caching
- Integration
- Composite

17. What is hybrid cloud architecture?

Hybrid cloud architecture is that cloud architecture which is using both public cloud and any private servers on your premises. This architecture
Can be established by including public virtual servers on virtual private cloud and connecting that virtual cloud with your premises servers using a VPN (Virtual private network).

18. What are pros and cons of hybrid cloud?

Pros:

- Scalability
- Cost effective
- Security
- Flexibility

Cons:

- Infrastructure dependency
- Networking
- Security compliance

19. Explain the concept of Windows Azure diagnostics?

Windows Azure diagnostics is the service for storing the diagnostics data either in the table or in a blob. For collecting this stored diagnostics data, Windows Azure Diagnostics Monitor must be initialized.

Following is the diagnostic data which is stored in table storage:

- Data Source: Windows Azure Logs
  Table Name: WADLogsTable

- Data Source: Windows Azure Diagnostics
  Infrastructure Logs

Table Name:
WADDiagnosticInfrastructureLogsTable

- Data Source: Windows Event logs
  Table Name:
  WADWindowsEventLogsTable

- Data Source: Performance counters
  Table Name:
  WADPerformanceCountersTable

Following is the diagnostic data which is stored in blob storage:

- Data Source: IIS Logs
- Container Name: wad-iis-logfiles

- Data Source: Failed Request Logs
- Container Name: wad-iis-failedreqlogfiles

- Data Source: Crash Dumps
- Container Name: wad-crash-dumps

20. What are Microsoft Azure Queries?

Microsoft azure Queries provides loose connectivity between various components. It maintains a queue as a connector for connecting the two components. It is basically a service for storing large amount of transferred message data.

21. What are the drawbacks of using Microsoft Azure Queries?

There are also some drawbacks of using Microsoft Azure Queries, these are:
- Queues incurred some extra charges, although these are minimal charges.
- Queue is here working as a mediator, but if queue is down, then devices and components will be unable to communicate with each other.

22. How Queues can be created in storage account?

Here are the steps for creating queues in storage account:
- FIFO implementation
- Messages to be transferred will added to the end of the queue but will processed from the front.
- There are supported good ways by queue services for front end and back end decoupling.

23. Explain the key concepts of the tables in Microsoft Azure Service?

Table is used as storage way for facilitating data storage. Here are the key concepts of the tables in Microsoft Azure Service:

- Tables supports a structured and well-organized data storage.
- Collection of entities are stored in a table.
- Entities properties are specified in key-value pair.
- Entities are stored in tables.
- In one storage account, it can contain n number of tables.

24. Explain how messages can be send and received through Queue?

Send Messages to Queue:

Messages can be send using the CreateFromConnectionString API Call.
Here is the example demonstrating sending of messages:

```
string connectionstring =
CloudConfigurationManager.GetSetting
("Microsoft.ServiceBus.ConnectionStr
ing");

QueueClient Client =
```

```
QueueClient.CreateFromConnectionStri
ng(connectionString,
"TestExampleSendQueue");

Client.Send(new BrokeredMessage());
```

Receive Messages from Queue:

Messages can be received from a queue by operating the queue object in two different modes:
- ReceiveAndDelete
- PeekLock

Here is the example demonstrating receiving of messages:

```
Client.Receive();

while (true)

{

    BrokeredMessage message =
    Client.Receive();

    if (message != null)

    {

        try

        {

            Console.WriteLine("Body: "
            + message.GetBody < string
            > ());
```

```
        Console.WriteLine("Message
        ID: " +
        message.MessageId);

        Console.WriteLine("Test
        Property: " +
        message.Properties["TestPr
        operty"]);

        message.Complete();
    }
    catch (Exception)
    {
        message.Abandon();
    }
    }
}
```

25. What are the various storage available in Windows Azure?

There are basically three storages available in Windows Azure:
- BLOB
- Table
- Queue

26. What is Windows Azure Traffic Manager?

Windows Azure Traffic Manager supports the features of allowing users to control the distribution of their send traffic across various deployed Azure cloud computing services. There are following options available for configuring the Windows Azure Traffic Manager:
• DNS Name
• DNS Time to Live
• Load Balancing Method
• Monitoring Setting

27. What are the various load balancing methods available in Microsoft Azure service?

There are basically three load balancing methods available in Microsoft Azure service:
• Performance
• Round-Robin
• Failover

28. Explain the features of Windows Azure Traffic Manager?

Here are the listed benefits of Windows Azure Traffic Manager:
- Increase Performance
- High Availability
- No Downtime Required for Upgrade and Maintenance
- Easy to configure

29. What are the data synchronization ways available in Microsoft Azure Service?

There are basically available two ways of synchronization of data in Microsoft Azure Service:
- Synchronize an SQL Azure database from one SQL Azure server to another SQL Azure server.
- Synchronize an SQL Azure Database from an Azure Server to a Local Server database.

30. Explain the security management system of SQL Azure?

SQL Azure Security management system consist of following:
- Logins
- Users
- Schemas

- Roles
- Permissions

31. Name the different types of databases in SQL Azure?

There are basically two types of databases in SQL Azure:
  - Web Edition Relational Database
  - Business Edition DB

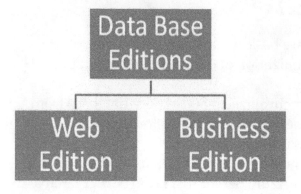

32. Explain the concept of Virtual Machine in Microsoft Azure Service?

Azure Virtual Machine have a significant role to play when you want frequent modifications in your existing web server environment.

It supports a rich set of features but configuring, maintaining and securing the azure Virtual Machine requires much more expertise and time as compared to other azure Web Services.

33. How Virtual Machine can be created in Azure Platform?

Here are the following steps for creating a virtual machine in Azure Platform:
1) Login to the Azure Management Portal.
2) Click on New.
3) Select compute.
4) Select Virtual Machine.
5) Select 'From Gallery'.
6) Select the operating system on which virtual machine has to be installed.
7) Fill the user details, VM RAM, VM name and required number of cores.
8) Fill cloud configuration and DNS setting details.
9) Create end points for accessing virtual machine.
10) Now VM is created and will be running within few minutes. It can be seen through the Azure portal.

34. What is autoscaling application in Azure?

Autoscaling application blocks are used for automatically scaling the Windows Azure application based on some set of rules specified by the running application.
There are two such types of rules specified:
• Constraint rule
• Reactive rules

35. Explain the concept of AWS Cloud Formation?

AWS Cloud Formation is a cloud builder service for modeling and setting up the AWS resources thereby it will reduce the time spend on managing these resources, rather than this, time can be utilized further for focusing on these AWS applications.
AWS cloud formation incurred no additional charges.
There are basically two main parts of AWS Cloud Formation:
• Cloud Formation Template
• Cloud Formation Stack

36. What is profiling in Azure?

Profiling refers to the process of measuring the performance analysis of an application. It is used for ensuring the stability of a running application and able to sustain high traffic.

Here are the uses of obtained profiling reports:

- Determine the most time-taking and longest method within the running application.
- Evaluation of memory allocation.
- Analysis of concurrency issues.
- Measurement of execution time associated with each method in the call stack.

37. What are the steps of connecting an Azure Hosted website to FTP?

Here are the listed steps for connecting an Azure Hosted website to FTP:

- Stop
- Restart
- Manage Domains
- Delete
- Web Matrix

38. What is Cmdlet in Azure Service?

A cmdlet is a lightweight command used in the Microsoft command-line interface. It is written in .NET programming language.

It is used for handling the object inputs and outputs using object-based pipeline. All the available Cmdlets and functions can be queried by using,

Get-Command Cmdlet.

39. What is Azure Explorer?

Azure Explorer is one of the free Microsoft Azure Storage Tool for managing all Microsoft Azure blobs. It is a useful GUI tool for inspection and alternation of data.

40. What is Service Fabric in Azure?

Azure Service Fabric refers to next-generation middleware cloud computing platform for building scalable and reliable enterprise applications.
Here are the features of Azure Service Fabric:
- Development of Scalable Applications
- Development of Stateless and Stateful services
- Deploying applications within the seconds
- Deploying different versions of same applications
- Managing the entire life-cycle of stateful applications

41. Name the components of cloud computing architecture?

There are four main components of cloud computing architecture:
- Front-end device
- Back-end platform
- Cloud-based delivery
- Network

42. What are the replication options available in Azure Storage Account?

There are four replication options available in Azure Storage Account:
- Locally redundant storage
- Zone-redundant storage
- Geo-redundant storage
- Read-access geo-redundant storage

43. What are Blobs? What are types of Blobs?

Blobs refers to 'Binary Large Object'. These are storage type available for storing images, audios, videos and text files.
There are three types of Blobs:
- Block blobs
- Append blobs

- Page blobs

44. Write command for deletion of Queue?

```
Queue can be deleted by using
below command syntax,


$QueueName = "TestQueue"

Remove-AzureStorageQueue –Name
$QueueName-Context $Ctx
```

45. Write command for CRUD operations on Azure table?

Here is the specified command for performing CRUD operations on Azure table using Windows Command shell:

- **Creating a Table:**

  ```
  $tabName = "TableName"
  New-AzureStorageTable –Name $tabName
  –Context $Ctx
  ```

- **Retrieve Table**

  ```
  $tabName = "TableName"
  ```

```
Get-AzureStorageTable –Name $tabName
–Context $Ctx
```

- **Delete Table**

```
$tabName = "TableName"
Remove-AzureStorageTable –Name
$tabName –Context $Ctx
```

46. Explain the concept of Microsoft Azure–CDN?

Microsoft Azure–CDN is a content delivery system for putting the stuffs like blobs and other static content in a cache. Thereby, it provides maximum bandwidth while delivering the content to the uses across cloud computing platform.

Here are the steps for creating a CDN:

- Login in to your Azure Management Portal
  - Click New
  - Select APP Services
  - Select CDN
  - Click Quick Create
  - There fields in popup will come: -
    ➤ Subscription
    ➤ Origin Type
    ➤ Origin URL

- Choose any one of the options
- Click Create
- CDN endpoint will thereby be created

47. Write the command for installing Azure CLI on windows and Linux?

Azure CLI installation command on Windows:

pip install --user azure-cli

Azure CLI installation command on Linux:

curl -L https://aka.ms/InstallAzureCli | bash

48. What are the different options for managing the session state in windows Azure?

There are three different options for managing the session state in windows Azure:

➢ Windows Azure Caching
➢ SQL Azure
➢ Azure Table

49. What are the available instance sizes of Azure Virtual Machine?

The available instance sizes of Azure Virtual Machine are as follows:

- Compute Instance Size
  Extra Small

- CPU Memory
  Ghz

- Instance Storage
  768 MB

- I/O Performance
  20 GB Low

- Compute Instance Size
  Small

- CPU Memory
  1.6 GHz

- Instance Storage
  1.75 GB

- I/O Performance
  225 GB Moderate

- Compute Instance Size
  Medium

- CPU Memory
  2 x 1.6 GHz

- Instance Storage

3.5 GB

- I/O Performance
  490 GB High

- Compute Instance Size
  Large

- CPU Memory
  4 x 1.6 GHz

- Instance Storage
  7 GB

- I/O Performance
  1,000 GB High

- Compute Instance Size
  Extra large

- CPU Memory
  8 x 1.6 GHz

- Instance Storage
  14 GB

- I/O Performance
  2,040 GB High

50. What are the benefits of a cloud?

Here are the listed benefits of a cloud:
- Lower costs
- Software updates
- Backups

- Data hosted centrally
- Scalability
- Fail over
- Monitoring services
- Data storage

51. Explain the differences between public cloud and private cloud?

Here are the listed differences between public cloud and private cloud:

Public Cloud:

- Pay for the resources that are being used and whenever you require them.
- Public cloud is provided for commercial use.
- Able to supports heavy workloads.
- Cheapest for users.
- Scalable.
- Better resources optimization as no wastage of resources.

Private Cloud:

- Expensive
- Automated Security Features

- Much similar in features as that of public cloud except security and maintenance features
- Owned by specific individual or private group
- Highly Controlled

52. What is Storage Keys?

Storage keys are also known as Access Keys, used for authentication of storage services account for facilitation manipulation of associated information based on their respective accounts.

53. What is Federation in SQL Azure?

Federation main purpose in SQL Azure is scalability, by helping both administrators and developers for facilitating the scalability of organized data.
It supports basic scaling of data objects in SQL Azure database. These Federations are basically the partitioned data, and there can be multiple federations within the database and each federation will have their own distribution schema.
A Federation Object Contains:
- Distribution Schema and Range

- Distribution Key
- Data Type

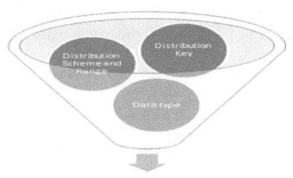

Federation Object

54. What are the SQL Azure Firewall Rules?

SQL Azure Firewall Rules are provided for data protection and preventing the access restrictions to the SQL Azure database. These accessed to SQL Azure database are blocked or authorized by these firewall rules.

55. Explain the Web Edition Relation Database?

A Web Edition Relation Database typically includes:

- 5 GB of a T-SQL based relational database
- Self-managed DB
- Auto high availability
- Fault tolerance
- Suitable for Web applications and other custom applications
- Supports tools such as Visual Studio, SSIS, BCP etc.

56. Explain the Business Edition Database?

A Business Edition Database typically includes:
- 50 GB of T-SQL based relational database
- Self-managed DB
- Auto high availability
- Fault tolerance
- Additional features like auto-partition, fanouts, CLR, etc.
- Supports tools such as Visual Studio, SSIS, BCP, etc.
- Suitable for Web applications and other custom applications and other Departmental applications

57. What us TFS build system in Azure Cloud Architecture/

TFS build system is basically an output of a solution, a file is available in. cspkg extension. TFS build systems includes following components:

- Build Servers
- Build Controllers
- Build Agents
- Build Definitions

58. Explain the concept of Good Cloud Platform?

Good Cloud Platform is new technology for using the cloud computing platform in real time. It is developed by the google developers team for giving the chance to other developers to host their cloud storage and web API's on the cloud computing infrastructure internally in the google products that includes google search, google play store, Gmail and You Tube.
Here are the listed set of cloud based services offered by Good Cloud Platform:

- Hosting and computing
  - App Engine
  - Compute Engine
- Cloud storage
  - Cloud Storage
  - Cloud Store
  - Cloud SQL

- BigData
  - ➤ BigQuery
- Services
  - ➤ Cloud Endpoints
  - ➤ Translate API
  - ➤ Prediction API

59. What is VM role?

VM Role is a Role in Azure Platform for maintaining service packs, patches and other web applications that are already being installed. VM Role is used in following Cases:
- Long-Running Setup
- Error-Prone Application

60. What is Windows Azure Scheduler?

Windows Azure Scheduler are the automated scheduled cron jobs run for automating the actions and posting the messages to a storage queue as per the scheduled time.
Scheduling provides entire history details of the apps configured within the cloud such as its status, start time, end time information, etc.

61. Why do you go with Microsoft Azure Platform?

There are many regions for using and running the Microsoft Azure Platform:

- Flexibility
- Extendable
- Scalable
- Protection
- Trusted

62. What are different types of storage account provided by Azure Storage Providers?

There are basically two types of storage account provided by Azure Storage Providers:

- **Standard Storage Account**

  Supported Storage Types:

  ➢ Blob STORAGE
  ➢ Table STORAGE
  ➢ Queue STORAGE

- **Premium Storage Account**

  Supported Storage Types:

  ➢ Azure Virtual Machine Disks

63. What is Automated Assessment and Migration tool in Microsoft Azure?

The Automated Assessment and Migration tool in Microsoft Azure offers following listed features:
- Provide a high level readiness assessment
- Used in report outlines sites
- Provided detailed reports which offers expertise guidance
- Tool can create any website and their associated databases automatically and thereby auto-synchronizing the content as well

64. Explain the concept of Azure Mobile Engagement?

Azure Mobile Management refers to the SAAS-delivered and data driven user engagement platform for enabling real-time notifications across all connected devices.
Here are the functionalities supported by Azure Mobile Engagement:
- Real Time analytics for increasing the usage of Azure Apps
- Push Notification
- Open API's
- Easily integration

- Data Protection
- Data Privacy

65. What is WordPress in Microsoft azure Platform?

WordPress in Microsoft azure Platform refers to the web software for creation of websites, web apps and blogs.
This web software is built by hundreds of community volunteers and there are thousands of available plugins and themes that has been developed.

66. What is Azure HDInsight?

Azure HDInsight refers to feature supported for ensuring deployment and provision of Apache Hadoop clusters within the cloud.
It provides a software framework that has been designed for managing, analyzing and reporting the big data statistics.

67. What are the various options available for creating an HDInsight Cluster in Azure Platform?

There are following options available for creating a HDInsight Cluster in Azure Platform:
- Hadoop is a default implementation of apache Hadoop.
- Storm is an open source system for processing data in real time.
- HBase is an open source NoSQL database built on Hadoop for providing random access and consistency of large amount of unorganized and unstructured data.

68. What are the steps for enabling remote desktop on the HDInsight cluster in Azure Platform?

Here are the listed procedural steps for enabling remote desktop on the HDInsight cluster in Azure Platform:
- Click HDInsight.
- List of available HDInsight clusters will be visible.
- Click the one of them HDInsight cluster for which you want to make a connection.
- Click configuration on the top.
- Click ENABLE REMOTE on the bottom.

69. What is Text Analytics API in Azure?

Text Analytics API refers to text analytics web services built for Azure   Machine Learning. This API returns Boolean values, i.e. numeric score between 0 and 1.
Here, Score 0 represents positive sentiment,
While score 1 represents negative sentiment.

70. What is Windows Azure Compute Emulator?

Windows Azure Compute Emulator is a local emulator used for building and testing the application before deploying these applications to the Windows Azure Platform.

71. What is Cspack?

Cspack refers to command-line tool for generating a service package file having. cspkg extension and preparing the application for deployment to Windows Azure or either to Windows Azure Compute Emulator.

72. What is Csrun?

Csrun refers to the command-line tool for deploying a packaged application to the Windows Azure Compute Emulator and thereafter managing the running service.

73. How Azure Worker Role Instances can be programmatically scale out?

Azure Worker Role Instances can be programmatically scale out using AutoScaling Application Block.

74. What are the steps of creating an Active Directory in Microsoft Azure?

Active Directory in Microsoft Azure can be created by using below steps:
- Sign in to Azure Management Portal
- Click New
- Click App Services
- Click Active Directory
- Click Directory
- Click Custom Create
- Provides the details such as a domain name
- After directory being created, it will have mapped with that domain

75. What are the steps of mapping custom domain in Microsoft Azure?

Custom domain can be mapped in Microsoft Azure through following below steps:
- See the list of directories
- Click on a directory name

- Click on 'Domain' that you want to map
- Click on Add a custom domain
- Provides the details that are required to fill in the popup screen
- Select single sign in option

76. Explain the code demonstrating handling of connection failure in Windows Azure?

Here is the example demonstrating handling of connection failure in Windows Azure:

```
static RetryPolicy policy = new
RetryPolicy(5,
TimeSpan.FromSeconds(2),
TimeSpan.FromSeconds(2));

    policy.ExecuteAction(() =>

        {

            try

            {

                string federationCmdText =
                @"USE FEDERATION
                Customer_Federation
                (ShardId =" + shardId + ")
                WITH RESET, FILTERING=ON";

                customerEntity.Connection.
                Open();
```

```
customerEntity.ExecuteStor
eCommand(federationCmdText
);


    }
    catch (Exception e)
    {
        customerEntity.Connection.Cl
        ose();
        SqlConnection.ClearAllPools(
        );
    }
});
```

77. What is DeadLetter Queue?

DeadLetter queue contains the messages in following scenarios:
  • When message expires, then expired messages deadletting is set to true.
  • When the max delivery count for a message is exceeded.
  • When a filter evaluation exception occurs, then messages deadletting is set to true.

78. How Alert rules can be set up in Microsoft Azure?

Here are the steps for setting up the Alert Rules in Microsoft Azure:

- Go to Monitoring Section of your Azure VM
- Select those metrics for which alert rules has to be set up
- Select Add Rule option from the bottom
- Enter the Alert Name and other requested information required in the Pop-up form
- Select Condition, can be either greater than, less than or equal
- Enter a threshold value (will specified in percentages)
- Maximum 10 alert rules can be set per subscription

79. What are the factors for choosing the Right Data Center for Azure application?

Choosing the Right Data Center for Azure application depends on three main factors:

- Performance
- Cost
- Legal Aspect

80. How you can create the Backup Vault in Microsoft Azure?

Backup Vault in Microsoft Azure can be creating using below steps:
- Login into Azure management portal
- Select New
- Select Data Services
- Select Recovery Services
- Select Backup Vault
- Select Quick Create
- Enter the Name of Backup Vault
- Select the Region
- Click Download Vault Credentials
- Click Download Agent
- Agents setup and Backup Vault Cred's will thereby save into your computer
- Click Proceed to Registration
- For Vault Identification, select the Vault Credential file from your computer
- Choose Generate Passphrase
- Save the Passphrase into a specific location into your computer
- Click on Next and Backup Vault Setup is thereby done

Chapter 3:

Job responsibilities of Azure Developer

Azure Cloud Developers have a wide role to play while working on cloud based applications development, configuration and deployment across cloud platform.

Here are the core job responsibilities of Azure Developer:

- Can Review the current cloud Architecture
- Knowledge of high-level design and code translation
- Expertise knowledge of Azure Cloud technologies and Azure web applications and Azure databases
- Worked with documentation of entire implementation and release plans of cloud development
- Adequate knowledge of Azure services and must be feasible in picking the right Azure service for the application.

- Be responsible for designing, maintenance, debugging and writing of clean code that optimize Azure performance and all other associated Azure web services that are being used by applications.
- Proven working experience in cloud computing, and, Azure architecture development.
- Creativity, good logical and technical skills, quick learning attitude.
- Strong teamwork skills, leadership skills and ability to handle project independently.
- Must possess a good knowledge about IAM roles, credentials, encryptions so to implement the code-level application security.
- Strong grasp of security, and cloud computing applications.
- Ability to deliver project within the constraints of timelines and project budgets.
- Ability to thrive in a fast-paced environment, quickly grasp the new and modern web technologies, mobile technologies and cloud computing technology and techniques.
- Problem solving attitude.
- Willingness to learn, debugging skills and possess a great passion for the work.

- Leveraging Azure SDK's for building feasible interaction of application with the Azure services

Chapter 4:

Tips on how to prepare for the interview

Interviews often brings up nervousness in the candidate mind. You should be well prepared with good confidence. While attending interview, candidate job is to convince the recruiter that you have the desired skills, knowledge and experience that you fit the organization's culture and job description.
Keep in mind, when you're interviewing for the job, little things and careful attention can make a big difference. Even a small mistake can result in losing the job opportunity that you may deserve. Confidence is the key towards achieving success. While attending interview, we all are nervous as it's the time when we have to prepare ourselves for facing the challenges, for giving us a chance to prove our skills and capabilities.
If you have enough confidence to handle a given job responsibilities, then you are on the right track. Don't worry your dream job is still yours.

A job interview gives you a chance to bright and show your talent. These tips are although sounds as smaller steps that you are thinking will have no impact on interview session, but believe me these have a key role to play. There are number of tips you should keep in mind to ensure that you make an impressive impression during the interview.

1. Analyze the job. Read carefully the job description and make a list of all skills, knowledge and experience that are required by the employer and are critical for success in the interview.

2. Before attending the job interview, it's important you should research the organization, their business tactics, their products and organization stability. This will help you to find out whether company and work culture are a good fit for you and will prove as a correct career move.

3. Spend your time to practice for the interview questions.

4. Revise the notes, all your quick learning short points, be handy with the basic questions answers as you won't be scrambling for an answer in front of the recruiter.

5. Look professional and sounds professional. Your dressing sensing and your body gesture will be a first impression in front of the recruiter and it will affect your impression for a further interview session.
6. Be on time, that means early. It shows your punctuality and your decent character. Try to relax and stay as calm as possible.
7. Pay attention while recruiter is asking questions, listen carefully as it will be embarrassing if you forget the question.
8. Carry relevant material to the interview.
9. Don't panic and be aware of your skills, capabilities and experience but don't lie about your skills and experience.
10. Don't be cocky. Attitude plays a key role in your interview success. You must maintain a fine balance between confidence, modesty and professionalism. Overconfidence is showing bad character.
11. Be careful while using social networking sites. Don't post too much on Facebook, LinkedIn or other social networking sites. Employers now usually keep following on these sites to gather information on prospective employees.
12. Have a good laugh, be positive, focused, candid, confident and concise.

13. Stick to your career plan, be your most authentic professional asset, act interested and never open a conversation with careless and negative remarks.
14. Always follow up with thank-you letter or note. If you interview with multiple peoples, send each one a personal note or a thank-you letter within 24 hours of your interview.
15. Stay motivated, if failed at once then it doesn't mean you are not eligible for success. Remember there are probably many applicants that appeared for the job and only a few of them will get the job. Try to learn from your mistakes and be better at the next interview.
16. Willingness to learn, quick grasping power and great enthusiasm.
17. Love your work, be determinant about your decisions.
18. Use right work, explain by giving good and reasonable examples in brief.
19. Be direct.
20. Share your accomplishments, highlights your good points, your strength and convince the hiring manager to make a mach.

Conclusion:

If you are looking to tackle the Azure interview smoothly with success, I hope above listed interview questions will help you a lot. These questions are for both the fresher's and experience candidates and get you on the right track of interview preparation.

When talking about Azure, you should have a good knowledge about cloud computing infrastructure and associated cloud computing applications configuration and deployment. One of the most important thing recruiters keep in mind while hiring developers is their creativity, developers who are constantly learning new things, expandable with the IT and software technology development. Their main aim is to understand how much developer has an understanding about the basic operations and well updated with the new language features. Azure programming has climbed rapidly. As, Cloud computing offers a wide range of opportunities and capabilities, open a new world covered with flexibility, platforms, services, applications and much more. Azure services are one of the best services supported by cloud platform. They must have to make the code much more responsive, cleaner, easily extensible and more optimized for performance.

Recruiters are in hunger of hiring such Azure developers that possess high quality programming skills, knows all the high and lows related to the web development process as it decides productivity and efficiency of project delivery to the client with satisfaction and within the predefined timeframe.

Practice and well preparation, research about the company organization, your attitude, confidence for your skills, abilities and experience, being updated about the IT revolution will play a vital role in improving your performance during an interview session. You can make your career path a little easier by adopting these smart tips, and no matter how you get interviewed for the job, over the phone, face-to-face, or among the group of candidates it will be stress free and exciting challenge.

Keep updated, keep learning, be confident and yes stay logical.

> *Good Luck Azure Developers.*
> *Enjoy while working with cloud setup, configuration, optimization and maintenance*
> *Keep learning, keep updated,*
> *It's all knowledge that matters at last.*